Cerebral Palsy

BY MICHELLE LEVINE

amicus
high interest

Amicus High Interest is an imprint of Amicus
P.O. Box 1329, Mankato, MN 56002
www.amicuspublishing.us

Library of Congress Cataloging-in-Publication Data
Levine, Michelle, author.
 Cerebral palsy / by Michelle Levine.
    pages cm. — (Living with—)
 Summary: "Describes what it is like to live with cerebral palsy,
what its symptoms are, and how it is treated"— Provided by
publisher.
 Audience: K to grade 3.
 Includes bibliographical references and index.
 ISBN 978-1-60753-482-2 (library binding) —
 ISBN 978-1-60753-695-6 (ebook)
 1. Cerebral palsy—Juvenile literature. 2. Cerebral palsy—
Treatment—Juvenile literature. I. Title.
 RJ496.C4L427 2015
 616.8'36—dc23
                                          2013034204

Editors   Kristina Ericksen and Rebecca Glaser
Series Designer   Kathleen Petelinsek
Book Designer   Heather Dreisbach
Photo Researcher   Kurtis Kinneman

Photo Credits: dbimages/Alamy, cover; Janine Wiedel
Photolibrary/Alamy, 5; Jeff Greenberg/Alamy, 6; ZUMA
Press, Inc./Alamy, 8; Domine/Shutterstock, 10;
CristinaMuraca/Shutterstock, 13; Paul Doyle/Alamy, 14;
Dorling Kindersley/Getty Images, 17; dbimages/Alamy, 18;
Jeff Greenberg/Alamy, 21; ZUMA Press, Inc./Alamy, 22;
Gallo Images/Alamy, 24; George S de Blonsky/Alamy, 27;
YAY Media AS/Alamy, 28

Printed in the United States of America at Corporate Graphics
in North Mankato, Minnesota.

10 9 8 7 6 5 4 3 2 1

Table of Contents

What Is Cerebral Palsy?

Do you know someone with **cerebral palsy**? Then you know it's called CP. This girl has CP. She has trouble using her legs. Her muscles are stiff. It's hard to bend or move them. It makes walking hard. But she goes to school just like you. And she enjoys many activities.

Cerebral palsy makes it
hard for this girl to move.

This boy uses a special keyboard.
It helps him communicate.

Q How many people in the United States have CP?

CP causes problems with muscles. It can make them stiff. It can make them shake or jerk. And it can cause poor balance or body control.

Different body parts can have problems. It may be legs. It may be arms. It may be half the body. It may be the whole body.

About 800,000 people have CP.

Some people with CP have trouble walking. They may not walk at all, so they use a wheelchair. Or they may walk with jerky movements. Others have trouble with their hands. Tying shoes is hard. So is holding things. Speaking is also difficult. So is chewing and swallowing.

Walkers help kids with cerebral palsy take part in activities such as skating.

Doctors use a special machine to take pictures of a person's brain.

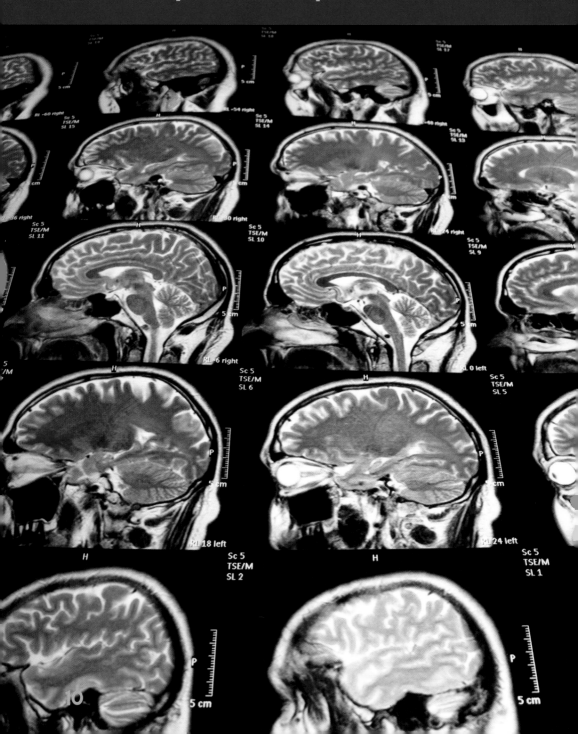

What Causes Cerebral Palsy?

CP is caused by a problem in the brain. The brain is very important. It is your body's boss. It sends messages to your muscles. It tells them what to do. Muscles let you walk, clap, and jump. They even make you smile.

The brain of someone with CP is different. It has trouble sending those messages. So the muscles don't work right.

Why are the brains of people with CP different? Their brains do not grow the right way. It often happens before they are born. Other people get CP later. Their brain gets hurt. Or a sickness harms it. Then the brain stops growing right.

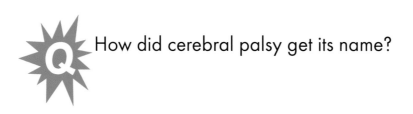
How did cerebral palsy get its name?

This is an ultrasound picture. It shows a baby before it has been born.

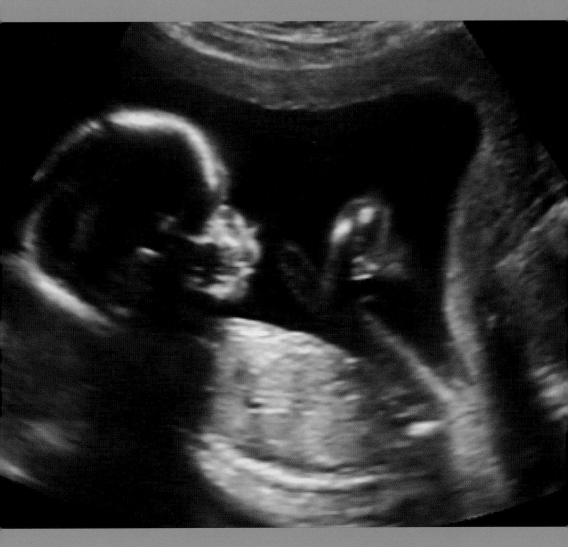

 Cerebral means brain. *Palsy* means problems with muscles.

Most people with cerebral palsy have stiff muscles. It hurts to move.

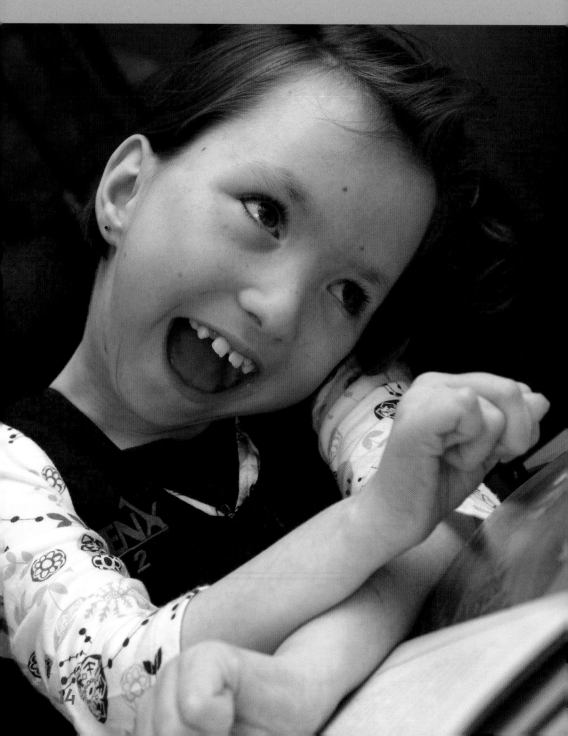

Types of Cerebral Palsy

There are three types of cerebral palsy. The most common one causes stiff muscles. Eight of ten people with CP have this type. The stiffness can be in the arms or legs. Or it can be in the whole body. The face can be stiff, too. Moving the muscles is hard. It can hurt.

Other types of CP are less common. One type makes it hard to use muscles. They do not stay still. They shake, jerk, and twist. Sitting and walking are hard. So are eating and swallowing.

The last type of CP causes problems with balance and movement. Walking is hard. So is grabbing things. Quick movements are hard, too.

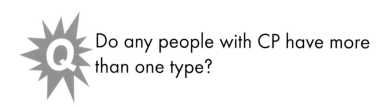
Do any people with CP have more than one type?

Some people cannot hold a spoon or fork well. They use special ones that are easier to grab and use.

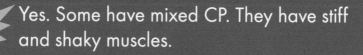

A Yes. Some have mixed CP. They have stiff and shaky muscles.

This boy works hard. He is making his muscles stronger.

Treating Cerebral Palsy

There is no cure for CP. It doesn't go away. A person with CP will have it for life. But there is help. Medicines can loosen stiff muscles. **Surgery** can, too. Most people with CP get **physical therapy**. It helps them control their bodies. It helps with walking and balance, too. And it makes speaking and eating easier.

Some people with CP have other problems. A common one is learning. Some people with CP are slow learners. New skills and ideas are hard for them. Teachers can help. Poor sight is also common for people with CP. So is weak hearing. Glasses and **hearing aids** can help.

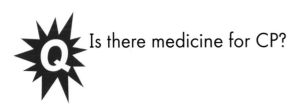
Is there medicine for CP?

**This boy needs extra help
to learn new things.**

 Yes. Medicine doesn't make it go away.
But it can help lessen muscle pain.

Living with Cerebral Palsy

Many people with CP use tools. Some wear **braces**. These stretch tight muscles. And they help with walking. So do **crutches**. Others use wheelchairs.

Some people with CP need tools for their hands. They use forks and spoons with special handles that are easier to hold. The handles fit on crayons and pencils too.

Leg braces help this boy play baseball.

This boy practices kicking a soccer ball. A walker helps him balance.

 Are there tools to help with speaking?

Kids with CP are like you. They like to be with friends. They like to have fun. Many kids with CP go to regular school. But some go to a special school. Teachers give them extra help.

 Yes! Some people with CP use special computers. They type words. Or they press pictures. The computer talks for them.

Many adults with CP lead full lives. They have homes and jobs. They get married. They have families. Others need more help. They live with their parents. Or they live in a **group home**. But CP doesn't stop them. They have friends and hobbies. And they are active.

Some people with cerebral palsy play in the Paralympics.

Do you have friends with CP? Tasks may be hard for them. Ask how you can help. And find fun things to do together. Play a game. Or go outside on a nice day. People with cerebral palsy enjoy many things, just like you!

You can help friends with cerebral palsy. You can have fun together.

Glossary

brace Something a person wears that supports or stretches a body part.

cerebral palsy A brain condition that causes problems with muscle movement.

crutch A walking tool that goes on or under a person's arm.

group home A home for people who need extra help with daily tasks, like people with CP.

hearing aid A small medical tool that goes inside the ear to help with hearing.

physical therapy Exercises and other activities that help with body movement.

surgery Something a doctor does inside a person's body to treat a problem.

Read More

Bjorklund, Ruth. *Cerebral Palsy.* New York: Marshall Cavendish Benchmark, 2007.

Levete, Sarah. *Explaining Cerebral Palsy.* Mankato, Minn.: Smart Apple Media, 2010.

Sheen, Barbara. *Cerebral Palsy.* Detroit: Lucent Books, 2012.

Websites

Kid's Health—Cerebral Palsy
kidshealth.org/kid/health_problems/brain/cerebral_palsy.html

The Royal Children's Hospital—Kid's Health Cerebral Palsy
www.rch.org.au/kidsinfo/fact_sheets/Cerebral_Palsy_an_overview/

Index

About the Author

Michelle Levine has written and edited many nonfiction books for children. She loves learning about new things—like cerebral palsy—and sharing what she's learned with her readers. She lives in St. Paul, Minnesota.